We go

We go to the library.

Grandfather's Journey
ANIMAL PARADE
TIDDALICK THE FROG
Ten Little Teddy Bears
Maureen Roffey
NURSE LUGTON'S CURTAIN
SNAIL MAIL
HARRY
THE VERY HUNGRY CATERPILLAR
PHOEBE GILMAN
Something from Nothing
TRACKS
PENGUIN
WHAT AM I?

We go to the park.

We go to the pool.

We go to the soccer game.

12

We go to the beach.

We go to the farm.

We go to the zoo.

We go to the aquarium.